# Cell Scientists:

From Leeuwenhoek to Fuchs

Summit Free Public Library

by Kimberly Fekany Lee

## MISSION: SCIENCE

**Science Contributor**
Sally Ride Science
**Science Consultants**
Thomas B. Ciccone, Science Educator
Ronald Edwards, Ph.D., Science Educator

# MISSION: SCIENCE

Developed with contributions from Sally Ride Science™

Sally Ride
Science

Sally Ride Science™ is an innovative content company dedicated to fueling young people's interests in science.

Our publications and programs provide opportunities for students and teachers to explore the captivating world of science—from astrobiology to zoology.

We bring science to life and show young people that science is creative, collaborative, fascinating, and fun.

To learn more, visit www.SallyRideScience.com

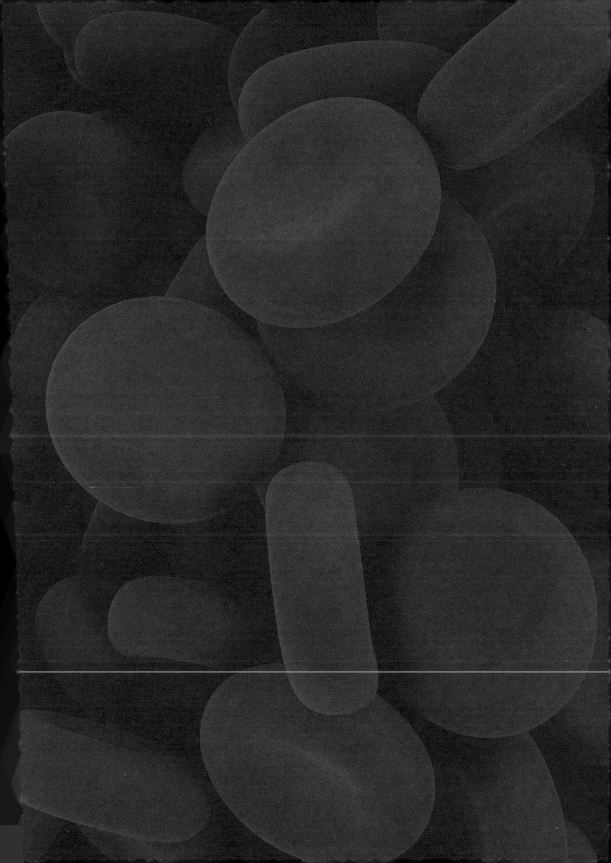

First hardcover edition published in 2009 by
Compass Point Books
151 Good Counsel Drive
P.O. Box 669
Mankato, MN 56002-0669

Editor: Jennifer VanVoorst
Designer: Heidi Thompson
Editorial Contributor: Sue Vander Hook

Art Director: LuAnn Ascheman-Adams
Creative Director: Keith Griffin
Editorial Director: Nick Healy
Managing Editor: Catherine Neitge

 This book was manufactured with paper containing at least 10 percent post-consumer waste.

Library of Congress Cataloging-in-Publication Data
Lee, Kimberly Fekany
  Cell scientists : from Leeuwenhoek to Fuchs / by Kimberly Fekany Lee.
    p. cm.—(Mission: Science)
  Includes index.
  ISBN 978-0-7565-3964-1 (library binding)
1.  Cytologists—Biography—Juvenile literature.  I. Title.
  QH26.L44 2009
  571.6092'2—dc22                              2008007729

Visit Compass Point Books on the Internet at *www.compasspointbooks.com*
or e-mail your request to *custserv@compasspointbooks.com*

# Table of Contents

# Cell Scientists

Human beings are naturally curious. We search, explore, and question. Curiosity has led to countless discoveries, inventions, and scientific breakthroughs. More than three centuries ago, scientists discovered the tiniest unit of life—the cell. They found it because they were interested in plants and animals. They wanted to learn more about living things.

Cells were too small for the human eye to see. Scientists needed something to make their samples look larger. They used an optical microscope, also known as a light microscope, which magnified their specimens about 20 to 30 times.

The discovery of the cell encouraged other scientists to learn more. Through the centuries, curious people discovered more and more about the cell— the basic structure of every living thing.

## Did You Know?

The microscope was developed in the early 1600s in the Netherlands. Three Dutch eyeglass makers— Hans Lippershey, Hans Janssen, and his son Zacharias—are credited with the invention. Experimenting with eyeglass lenses led them to their discovery.

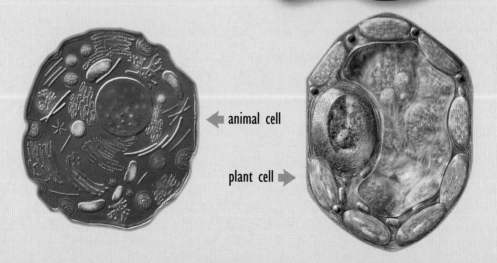

← animal cell

plant cell ➡

# Anton van Leeuwenhoek (1632-1723)

Anton van Leeuwenhoek is best known for the improvements he made to the microscope. He is also known for his cell research. He was born in Delft, the Netherlands, on October 24, 1632. Anton's father was a basket maker. His mother's relatives were brewers. At the age of 16, he became an apprentice to a Scottish cloth merchant in Amsterdam. He learned to buy and sell fabric.

At the age of 22, Leeuwenhoek returned to Delft and started his own business selling fabric. He also had other jobs. Some of them turned into businesses of their own.

It wasn't easy for Leeuwenhoek to become a scientist. His family didn't have a lot of money, and he didn't have a higher education. He knew only one language—Dutch—which was quite unusual for scientists of his time. But his curiosity was endless, and he worked hard. By the time Leeuwenhoek was 48, other scientists finally recognized him as an equal. He joined a special group of scientists called the Royal Society for the Improvement of Natural Knowledge.

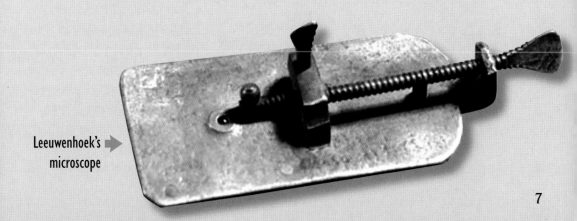

Leeuwenhoek's microscope

Leeuwenhoek had an important skill. He knew how to make things out of glass. This skill came in handy when he made lenses for his simple microscope. His one-lens microscopes were some of the best microscopes of the time.

Leeuwenhoek used his microscopes to study living organisms. He paid close attention to the things he saw and wrote down his observations. Since he couldn't draw well, he hired an artist to draw pictures of what he described. He saw tiny veins with blood flowing through them. He also saw living bacteria in pond water and on the surface of teeth.

Bacteria (blue specks) on the surface of a tooth

## Smile!

Leeuwenhoek made many interesting discoveries by studying plaque on teeth. He looked at the plaque on his own teeth and said it was as thick as batter. He also looked at plaque on two women's teeth (probably those of his wife and daughter) and two old men who had never cleaned their teeth. On the old men's teeth, he found more than he could imagine. Under his microscope, he observed lots of little things moving around—some swimming, some spinning, and some bending in curves. What he saw were live bacteria.

## Many Microscopes

Leeuwenhoek made more than 400 microscopes. They were quite advanced for that time. Some of them could magnify things 200 times. Other microscopes of his day did much less, magnifying things only 20 to 30 times.

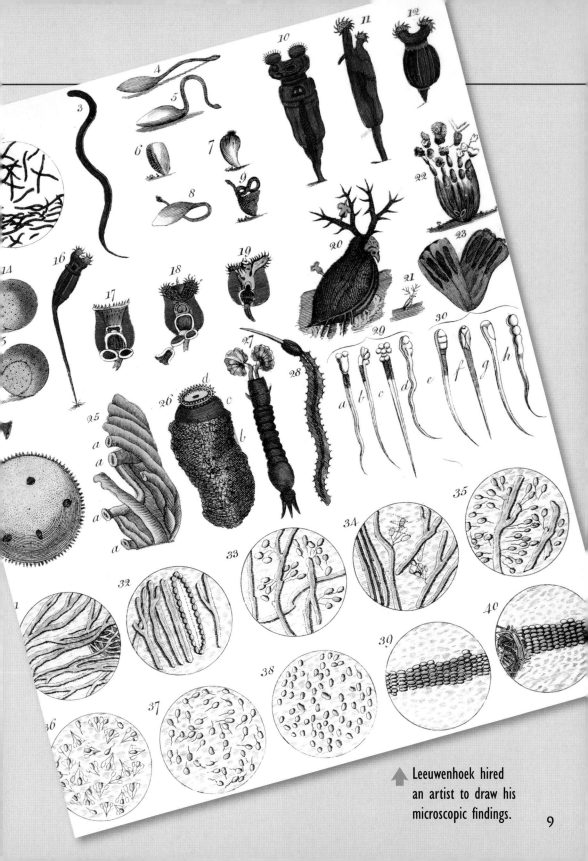

Leeuwenhoek hired an artist to draw his microscopic findings.

9

Robert Hooke was the first person to observe cells and give them their name. In 1665, at the age of 30, he made a compound microscope with three lenses. Then he placed a thin slice of cork under the microscope. Light from an oil lamp helped him see the sample, which was magnified about 30 times. Although the image wasn't clear, Hooke was able to see rows of tiny boxlike structures. They reminded him of the tiny rooms, or cells, that monks lived in. He named them *cellulae*, Latin for "little rooms." Hooke's curiosity led him to an important discovery. However, he didn't understand at that time how important cells were to the study of living things.

Robert Hooke began his life on July 18, 1635, in Freshwater on the Isle of Wight in England. Robert was a very smart child. As a young boy, he got smallpox, which left him scarred both physically and emotionally. He took refuge from his pain in scientific and mechanical pursuits, which had interested him from a very early age.

## Have You Seen It?

Robert Hooke created a book called *Micrographia*. In it, he drew detailed images of his observations through a microscope. His handmade leather and gold-tooled microscope is on display at the National Museum of Health and Medicine in Washington, D.C.

As a student at Oxford University, Hooke became an assistant to physicist Robert Boyle. Together, they made an air pump. In 1662, Hooke was appointed curator of experiments for the Royal Society, an important group of scientists. He used chemistry, anatomy, and biology in his experiments. It was a job he kept for 41 years. He made his famous cell discovery while working for the Royal Society.

Although Hooke led a successful life, he was not very happy or secure. His scars and deformities grew worse with age, and he was always in pain. Many people avoided him, while others made fun of him. Hooke died alone, blind, and bedridden on March 3, 1703. He was 67 years old.

The Great Fire of London in 1666 raged for nearly one full week. It destroyed about 80 percent of the city. Just a few people died, but thousands became homeless.

## Surveyor

Robert Hooke was a man with many skills. One of them was land surveying. His work as a surveyor was especially important to Londoners after the Great Fire of 1666. The fire wiped out large areas of the city. Hooke was in great demand and helped rebuild much of London.

# Matthias Schleiden (1804-1881)

# Theodor Schwann (1810-1882)

# Rudolf Virchow (1821-1902)

▲ Matthias Schleiden

▲ Theodor Schwann

▲ Rudolf Virchow

In the 1830s, three German scientists were studying cells at about the same time. They were Matthias Schleiden (a botanist), Theodor Schwann (a physiologist), and Rudolf Virchow (a medical doctor). Their discoveries became collectively known as the Cell Theory.

Schleiden was a lawyer who studied plants as a hobby.

Because he used a microscope to look at plants, he found that plants are made up of cells. His discovery became the first part of the Cell Theory: Plants are made up of one or more cells.

Schwann focused his research on animals. He discovered that, like plants, all animals are made up of cells. One night, Schwann and Schleiden had dinner together and talked about their work. They realized that the cells they both studied were very similar. Plants and animals were both made up of cells.

In 1839, Schleiden and Schwann published their findings. They made two important statements. First, all living things are made up of one or more cells. Second, a cell, which is alive, is the smallest part of a living thing.

The one thing they weren't sure of was where cells came from. Almost 20 years later, Rudolf Virchow solved the puzzle. He completed the Cell Theory with his discovery that cells come from other cells.

# Cell Theory

1. All living things are made from one or more cells.

2. The cell is the basic unit of life.

3. All cells come from pre-existing cells.

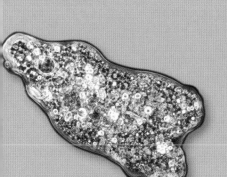

▲ single-celled organisms

▲ cell cross-section

▲ cell replication

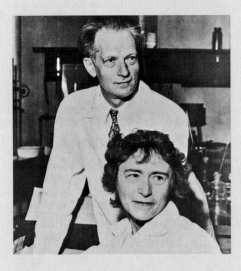

Gerty and Carl Cori are known for their work on anaerobic respiration, the cycling of molecules in the liver, the blood, and muscle cells to produce quick energy. In 1947, they received the Nobel Prize in medicine for their research in understanding this process, which is now known as the Cori cycle.

Gerty Theresa Radnitz was born on August 15, 1896, in Prague, Austria-Hungary (now the Czech Republic). She was home-schooled until the age of 10, when she was enrolled in a private girl's school. The schools for boys were different from girls' schools. Boys were challenged with literature, science, and math, while girls were taught manners and handicrafts so they could become young ladies.

Gerty, however, was interested in science and math, and she wanted to go to a university. First she had to attend a college-prep school and study science, math, and Latin. She completed the program in just two years and then enrolled in Charles University in Prague.

Carl Ferdinand Cori was born on December 5, 1896, in Prague, but he grew up in Trieste, Italy. Carl learned to love science at an early age, something fostered by his father and grandfather who were both scientists. When Carl was 18, the family moved back to Prague, where Carl began medical school at Charles University.

At the university, Carl met Gerty Radnitz. The two had a lot in common. They both liked hiking and mountain climbing. They also both wanted to be medical researchers. In 1920, Carl and Gerty graduated from the university. They also got married and started working together in medical clinics in Vienna, Austria.

World War I had ended just two years before the Coris graduated. Times were tough all over Europe, but they were especially hard for Jewish people, including Gerty Cori. There was a lot of prejudice, which made the Coris decide to move to the United States.

Carl Cori left before his wife to take a research job in Buffalo, New York. Six months later, Gerty Cori was hired by the same lab and joined her husband. After spending six years in the United States, the Coris became United States citizens.

After spending nine years in Buffalo, the Coris moved to St. Louis, Missouri. There Carl became a professor at the Washington University School of Medicine. Although Gerty had the same degree and the same years of experience as her husband, she was only made a research assistant. It took

## Prague

Today Prague is the capital and the largest city of the Czech Republic. The city is situated on the River Vltava and has a population of 1.2 million people. It is one of the most beautiful cities in Europe.

12 years for her to be offered a position as a professor.

The Coris did most of their research together. Most famously, they worked to understand the process of anaerobic respiration.

Cells need energy to work, repair themselves, and create new cells. They get that energy from a molecule called glucose. Normally glucose goes through a long process called aerobic respiration. The cell takes glucose and slowly pulls it apart. Each time a cell pulls a chunk off of a glucose molecule, energy is released. That energy is stored in a molecule called adenosine triphosphate (ATP).

When cells need quick energy, they use a process called anaerobic respiration. This process smashes glucose apart to create immediate energy. But anaerobic respiration produces less energy than aerobic respiration. It is also messy since it produces a byproduct called lactate.

Lactate is a molecule that still has energy inside it.

⬇ liver cells          ⬇ blood cells          ⬇ muscle cells

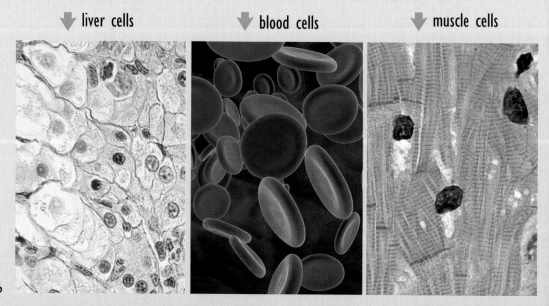

But the cell can't release it. Cells get rid of lactate molecules by dumping them into the bloodstream. The Coris wanted to know what happened to the lactate next.

They followed the lactate as the blood took it to the liver. Then the liver used six ATPs to change two lactate molecules into one glucose molecule. They called their findings the Cori cycle.

## Winners

As of 2007, 777 individuals and 20 organizations have been awarded the Nobel Prize. Only 34 of these were women. Besides the Coris, three other married couples share a Nobel Prize.

# The Cori Cycle

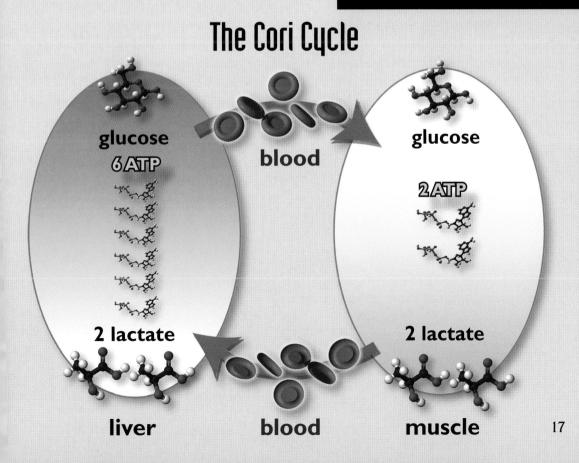

# Hans Adolf Krebs (1900-1981)

Hans Adolf Krebs was a medical doctor and biochemist who is known for his work on aerobic respiration. In 1953, he shared the Nobel Prize in medicine for his discovery of the Krebs cycle, the process by which cells turn glucose, or sugar, into energy that cells can use.

Hans Adolf Krebs was born in Hildesheim, Germany, on August 25, 1900, to Georg and Alma Krebs. His father was an ear, nose, and throat surgeon. Krebs studied medicine

and chemistry at several universities in Germany. Eventually he received a degree in medicine from the University of Hamburg.

In 1933, Adolf Hitler and the Nazi party took over Germany. They made it illegal for German Jews to work as doctors. So

Mitochondria are where aerobic respiration occurs.

Krebs, who was Jewish, left Germany and continued his work in England. Later he became a professor of biochemistry, the study of how molecules interact inside living things.

Krebs studied how cells get energy through aerobic respiration, a slow process that requires a lot of oxygen from the air we breathe. He discovered how the cell performs each step of aerobic respiration by taking glucose and slowly pulling it apart. He called this process the citric acid cycle, but it came to be known as the

Krebs cycle for the scientist who discovered it.

You already know about anaerobic respiration and the Cori cycle. That process creates quick energy, but it only produces two ATPs, or molecules that store energy, for every glucose molecule. The Krebs cycle takes a long time, but it produces much more energy—38 ATPs from one glucose molecule.

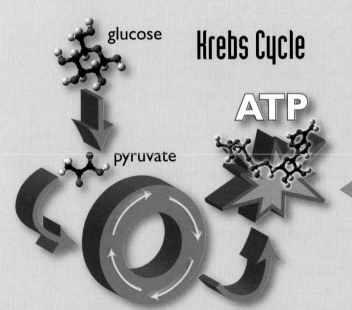

glucose

# Krebs Cycle

## ATP

pyruvate

Pyruvate is an intermediate molecule in the Krebs cycle.

▲ If you need a quick burst of energy, your cells use anaerobic respiration. It provides quick energy, but it leaves lactate in your muscles and blood.

To sum things up, cells have two ways to release energy from glucose: aerobic respiration and anaerobic respiration. Aerobic respiration (the Krebs cycle) takes a long time and requires oxygen, but it gets the most out of glucose—38 ATPs. Most of the time, your cells have time for aerobic respiration. But if you exert a lot of energy, you start breathing harder to get more oxygen for the Krebs cycle.

If you still need more energy, anaerobic respiration (the Cori cycle) kicks in.

It doesn't need oxygen. Anaerobic respiration breaks apart glucose to get less energy faster. Your cells can do it over and over again very quickly, providing quick bursts of energy. But this method leaves lactate behind. It also takes additional energy to turn the lactate back into glucose.

You have probably felt the difference while playing sports or exercising. You start breathing harder to get more oxygen for your cells. Once your cells use up all the oxygen you bring in, they start using

## Sore Muscles

Have you ever exercised so hard that you were sore afterward? Some biologists think that lactate is to blame. If your cells are using anaerobic respiration, they create a lot of lactate, which can build up in your muscle cells. There might be so much lactate that the cells bulge out and squeeze nerve cells.

Other biologists are not so sure that lactate is to blame. They don't think there is enough lactate to cause muscle cells to bulge. And besides, muscle soreness lasts longer than the lactate does. Once the blood carries the lactate to the liver, the aching should stop.

If you become a biochemist like Krebs and the Coris, perhaps you can find out what causes sore muscles.

anaerobic respiration. The process produces two ATPs very quickly, and your cells get the energy they need.

However, all that quick energy comes at a price. For every two ATPs it makes, it also makes two lactate molecules. These lactate molecules then go to the liver. The liver uses six more ATPs to change the two lactate molecules into one glucose molecule. So you get two ATPs right away, but later you have to use six more ATPs. In the end, anaerobic respiration means you lost four ATPs.

The important thing, however, is that you got the ATPs when you needed them. Imagine that you have just slid into home plate for the winning run. Or perhaps you have just sped down the field and kicked the soccer ball into the goal. After the run is made or the goal is scored, your body is still busy sending lactate to your liver, and your liver is busy converting lactate back into glucose. This is why you may feel tired or hungry after lots of exercise. Your cells are paying the price for all that anaerobic respiration!

# Rita Levi-Montalcini (1909-    )

Rita Levi-Montalcini is best known for discovering the chemicals in our bodies that help cells grow. She identified the nerve growth factor (NGF), the basis for cell growth. Her findings came from her research on chicken embryos. In 1986, at the age of 77, she received the Nobel Prize, which she shared with her research partner, Stanley Cohen.

Rita Levi-Montalcini was born on April 22, 1909, in Turin, Italy, one of four children. She and her twin sister were the youngest. Both of her parents were very cultured and educated. She described her family life as filled with love and devotion. It was a traditional family, and her father made the decisions. Although he respected women, he thought that a career would get in the way of being a wife and mother. His own two sisters had advanced degrees and found it hard to be wives and mothers while maintaining careers. For these reasons, he didn't allow his daughters to further their education.

Rita's twin sister didn't mind giving up a formal education. She was a

Turin is a beautiful city in northwest Italy. It is bordered on two sides by the Alps. In 2006, it was home to the Winter Olympic Games.

gifted artist and was able to pursue her goals without going to school. But it was difficult for Rita to accept her father's decision. She was a very intelligent person, and she had the ability to do extremely well.

Finally, when Rita was 20 years old, her father allowed her to work toward a professional career. She took Latin, Greek, and math, finishing high school in just eight months. Then she enrolled in medical school, graduating in 1936 at the top of her class and then becoming a medical doctor.

In a few years, World War II was being fought, and Jews were not allowed to practice medicine in Italy. Levi-Montalcini, who was Jewish, built a small secret lab in her bedroom. There she continued the research she had already begun on chicken embryos. When the war got worse, she moved her lab several times, first into a basement and then into the country.

Toward the end of the war, British and American forces hired Levi-Montalcini to work as a medical doctor. She cared for war refugees who were injured or ill. After the war, she became a professor in Turin until another researcher asked her to come to the United States. She joined him in St. Louis, Missouri, where they continued to experiment on chick embryos at Washington University. Though she became a professor of zoology and biology at Washington University, she spent much of her time in Rome, Italy, where she established another research facility.

In later years, she lived in Italy. The president of Italy made her a senator for life in the Italian Senate. It is a special honor that is given to a person for making an outstanding contribution in scientific, social, artistic, or literary fields.

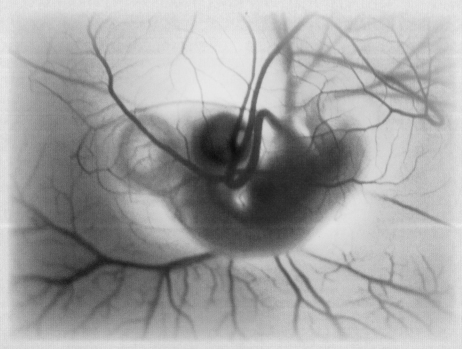

close-up of a chicken embryo

Stanley Cohen is a biochemist best known for the research he conducted with Rita Levi-Montalcini at Washington University in St. Louis, Missouri. Together, they discovered and studied chemicals in the body that stimulate cell growth. Those chemicals are often called growth factors. Cohen named their discovery epidermal growth factor, or EGF.

Stanley Cohen was born on November 17, 1922, in Brooklyn, New York. After receiving his bachelor's degree in chemistry and zoology, he worked as a bacteriologist at a milk processing plant. He went on to earn a master's degree in zoology. At the age of 26, he received a Ph.D. in biochemistry from the University of Michigan.

At Washington University, Cohen conducted research on cellular growth factors. This research has helped scientists understand how cancer develops. It has also aided in the design of anticancer drugs.

In 1959, Cohen became a professor of biochemistry at the Vanderbilt University School of Medicine in Nashville, Tennessee. Cohen has received several awards for his research, including the 1986 Nobel Prize that he shared with Levi-Montalcini.

# Joan Wright Goodman (1925-2006)

Joan Wright Goodman is known for her pioneering research on stem cells. A stem cell is a master cell in the human body with the ability to grow into any type of cell. Goodman paved the way for modern stem cell research when she identified stem cells in the blood of mice.

Joan Wright Goodman was born on May 14, 1925, in El Paso, Texas. She received a Ph.D. in physiology from the University of Rochester in New York. At Oak Ridge National Laboratory in Tennessee, she studied the effects of bone marrow transplants on fighting radiation damage. She also studied how cells respond to immunities— how the body fights infection and disease.

She then focused on isolating stem cells. Scientists knew that stem cells existed, but Goodman found stem cells in the blood. Goodman retired in 1985 at the age of 60. But she returned to the university and earned a law degree. After practicing law for just a short time, Goodman spent the remainder of her life supporting the arts in the San Francisco, California, area. She died on July 10, 2006, at the age of 81.

Throughout her life, Goodman encouraged women to become involved in science. She also encouraged all people to treat female scientists equally.

stem cells ➡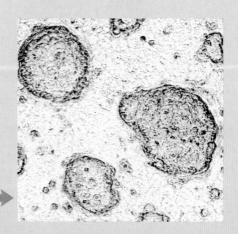

Christiane Nüsslein-Volhard is known for her research on genes that cause birth defects. She was born in Magdeburg, Germany, on October 20, 1942, during World War II. She was the second of five children. As a child, she was very interested in plants and animals, and she studied them with her family. By the age of 12, Christiane knew that she wanted to be a biologist. By the end of high school, she knew she wanted to be a researcher.

Although university classes bored her at first, Nüsslein-Volhard finally found a subject she was interested in: biochemistry. Only one university in Germany offered a program in that field, however. She left family and friends and went to school in Tübingen. She enjoyed her education there—especially a class on genetics.

After graduation, Nüsslein-Volhard worked in a laboratory studying DNA. DNA carries genetic

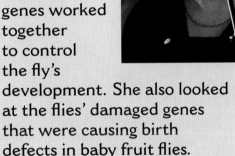

information for living things. Nüsslein-Volhard decided to study fruit flies. She learned that thousands of genes worked together to control the fly's development. She also looked at the flies' damaged genes that were causing birth defects in baby fruit flies.

Nüsslein-Volhard's work is important because it can be applied to human beings. In 1995, she received the Nobel Prize for her research.

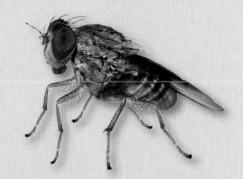

Fruit flies are the subject of ↑
Nüsslein-Volhard's research.

27

# Cell Biologist: Elaine Fuchs

## Rockefeller University

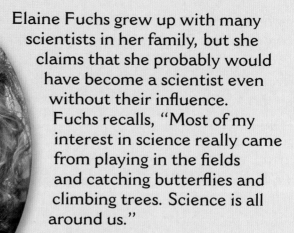

Elaine Fuchs grew up with many scientists in her family, but she claims that she probably would have become a scientist even without their influence. Fuchs recalls, "Most of my interest in science really came from playing in the fields and catching butterflies and climbing trees. Science is all around us."

Fuchs grew up just outside Chicago, Illinois. In 1972, she graduated from the University of Illinois with a bachelor's degree in chemical sciences. Then at Princeton

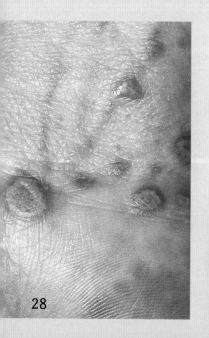

University in New Jersey, Fuchs earned her Ph.D. in biochemistry.

Fuchs studies the skin and hair of animals. Her research helps scientists understand how genes are involved in skin diseases. Fuchs also studies stem cells. Some stem cells have the ability to become skin, muscle, or even brain cells.

Fuchs has discovered how cells can either become skin or grow hair. One of Fuchs' projects is a super-fuzzy mouse that has much more hair than it should. Her discoveries may someday help treat people with skin diseases, baldness, or cancer.

"The most rewarding part of my job as researcher is the adventure of discovering something that no one else has known before," says Fuchs.

## Can You Find It?

"All we have to do is look at our own body and realize that science is a part of us," says Fuchs. Can you find any science in your body?

## Think About It

If you could treat any disease, what disease would you treat? What kinds of questions would you ask to get started?

Fuchs' research is working to make a difference for those battling skin diseases (from left), baldness, and skin cancer.

## Stanley Cohen

**Field of study:** *Biochemistry*
**Known for:** *Nerve growth factor*
**Nationality:** *American*
**Birthplace:** *Brooklyn, New York*
**Date of birth:** *November 17, 1922*

**Awards and honors:** *Nobel Prize in medicine, 1986; Louisa Gross Horwitz Prize from Columbia University, 1983; National Medal of Science, 1986*

## Carl Ferdinand Cori

**Field of study:** *Biochemistry*
**Known for:** *The Cori cycle*
**Nationality:** *Czech/American*
**Birthplace:** *Prague, Czech Republic*
**Date of birth:** *December 5, 1896*
**Date of death:** *October 20, 1984*

**Awards and honors:** *Albert Lasker Award for Basic Medical Research, 1946; Nobel Prize in medicine, 1947; shares a star on the St. Louis Walk of Fame with his wife, Gerty*

## Gerty Theresa Cori

**Field of study:** *Biochemistry*
**Known for:** *The Cori cycle*
**Nationality:** *Czech/American*
**Birthplace:** *Prague, Czech Republic*
**Date of birth:** *August 15, 1896*
**Date of death:** *October 26, 1957*

**Awards and honors:** *Became the third woman and the first American woman to win the Nobel Prize in medicine, 1947; the Cori crater on the moon is named for her; shares a star on the St. Louis Walk of Fame with her husband, Carl*

## Elaine Fuchs

**Field of study:** *Cell biology*

**Known for:** *Skin and skin disease research*

**Nationality:** *American*

**Birthplace:** *Chicago, Illinois*

**Awards and honors:** *Lounsbery Award from the National Academy of Sciences, 2001; Dickson Prize in Medicine from the University of Pittsburgh, 2004; FASEB Excellence in Science Award, 2006*

## Joan Wright Goodman

**Field of study:** *Stem cell research*

**Known for:** *Pioneering stem cell research*

**Nationality:** *American*

**Birthplace:** *El Paso, Texas*

**Date of birth:** *May 14, 1925*

**Date of death:** *July 10, 2006*

**Awards and honors:** *Award in her name established in her memory with the Association for Women in Science (AWIS)*

## Robert Hooke

**Field of study:** *Cell research*

**Known for:** *Observing and naming a cell; 41-year career as curator of experiments for the Royal Society*

**Nationality:** *English*

**Birthplace:** *Freshwater, Isle of Wight, England*

**Date of birth:** *July 18, 1635*

**Date of death:** *March 3, 1703*

**Awards and honors:** *Craters on the moon and on Mars are named in his honor; the Hooke Medal, awarded annually by the British Society for Cell Biology, was named in his honor*

## Hans Adolf Krebs

**Field of study:** *Biochemistry*
**Known for:** *The Krebs cycle*
**Nationality:** *German*
**Birthplace:** *Hildesheim, Germany*
**Date of birth:** *August 25, 1900*
**Date of death:** *November 22, 1981*

**Awards and honors:** *Nobel Prize in physiology, 1953; knighted in 1958*

## Anton van Leeuwenhoek

**Field of study:** *Cell research*
**Known as:** *Father of microbiology*
**Known for:** *Improvements to the microscope; discovering bacteria*
**Nationality:** *Dutch*
**Birthplace:** *Delft, the Netherlands*
**Date of birth:** *October 24, 1632*
**Date of death:** *August 30, 1723*

**Awards and honors:** *Research using the microscope was published by the Royal Society in its journal,* Philosophical Transactions; *appointed a fellow of the Royal Society, 1680*

## Rita Levi-Montalcini

**Field of study:** *Neurology*
**Known for:** *Nerve growth factor*
**Nationality:** *Italian*
**Birthplace:** *Turin, Italy*
**Date of birth:** *April 22, 1909*

**Awards and honors:** *Nobel Prize in medicine, 1986; National Medal of Science, 1987; named senator for life in Italian Senate*

## Christiane Nüsslein-Volhard

**Field of study:** *Biology*

**Known for:** *Genetic/DNA research*

**Nationality:** *German*

**Birthplace:** *Magdeburg, Germany*

**Date of birth:** *October 20, 1942*

**Awards and honors:** *Gottfried Wilhelm Leibniz Prize, 1986; Nobel Prize in medicine, 1995*

## Matthias Schleiden

**Field of study:** *Botany*

**Known for:** *Cell Theory*

**Nationality:** *German*

**Birthplace:** *Hamburg, Germany*

**Date of birth:** *April 5, 1804*

**Date of death:** *June 23, 1881*

**Awards and honors:** *Appointed professor of botany at the University of Dorpat in 1863*

## Theodor Schwann

**Field of study:** *Physiology*

**Known for:** *Cell Theory, Schwann cells*

**Nationality:** *German*

**Birthplace:** *Neuss, Germany*

**Date of birth:** *December 7, 1810*

**Date of death:** *January 11, 1882*

**Awards and honors:** *The cells he discovered, Schwann cells, share his name*

## Rudolf Virchow

**Field of study:** *Pathology*

**Known as:** *Father of pathology*

**Known for:** *Cell Theory*

**Nationality:** *German*

**Birthplace:** *Schiverbein, Germany*

**Date of birth:** *October 13, 1821*

**Date of death:** *September 5, 1902*

**Awards and honors:** *Copley Medal from the Royal Society of London, 1892*

# Glossary

**aerobic respiration**—slow process through which cells get energy

**anaerobic respiration**—process through which cells get energy quickly

**anatomy**—scientific study of the body and how its parts are arranged

**ATP**—adenosine triphosphate; molecule that stores energy

**bacteria**—single-celled microscopic creatures that exist everywhere in nature

**bacteriologist**—scientist who studies bacteria, especially in relation to medicine

**biochemistry**—study of chemical substances and vital processes occuring in living organisms

**biology**—science of living organisms

**bone marrow**—soft, fatty substance in the cavities of bones in which red blood cells are produced

**botanist**—biologist specializing in the study of plants

**cell**—smallest unit of living things

**Cell Theory**—states that all living things are made up of one or more cells, cells are the basic unit of life, and all cells come from other cells

**chemistry**—branch of science dealing with the structure, composition, and properties of substances and how they combine and change

**Cori cycle**—cycling of molecules in the liver, the blood, and muscle cells to produce quick energy; anaerobic respiration

**DNA**—deoxyribonucleic acid; molecule of which genes are made

**embryo**—animal organism in its early stages of development

**epidermal**—having to do with the outer layer of cells covering an organism

**gene**—basic unit of heredity

**genetics**—branch of biology that studies heredity and genetic variations

**glucose**—molecule that cells use to make energy

**growth factors**—chemicals that stimulate cell growth

**inheritance**—things received from an ancestor

**knighthood**—rank of a knight; an award given for special service or contribution

**Krebs cycle**—sequence of reactions by which most living cells generate energy during the process of aerobic respiration

**lactate**—molecule that is a byproduct of anaerobic respiration

**molecule**— small bit of matter made of two or more atoms bonded together

**monks**—men who live in a monastery to devote themselves to their religious vows

**nutrients**—substances, such as vitamins, that plants and animals need for good health

**physicist**—scientist who studies physics, the science of matter, energy, force, and motion

**physiologist**—scientist who studies living organisms

**prejudice**—hatred or unfair treatment of people who belong to a certain social group, such as a race or religion

**radiation**—emission of energy waves

**smallpox**—contagious viral disease that causes people's skin to break out in blisters and leaves deep scars

**stem cell**—type of cell that can give rise to any other kind of cell

**surveyor**—person who measures distance and angles in order to map land features

**zoology**—scientific study of animals

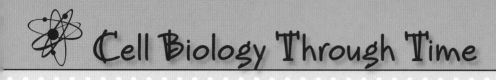

# Cell Biology Through Time

| | |
|---|---|
| **1665** | Robert Hooke views cell structure of cork under a microscope |
| **1683** | Anton van Leeuwenhoek discovers bacteria cells by studying tooth plaque |
| **1837** | Jan Evangelista Purkyne observes small granules (cells) while looking at a plant through a microscope |
| **1838** | Matthias Schleiden finds that plants are made up of cells |
| **1839** | Theodor Schwann discovers protective cells on nerve extensions; he calls them Schwann cells |
| **1844** | Karl Nägeli sees the process of cell growth and division under a microscope |
| **1855** | Rudolf Virchow states that all living cells come from other living cells |
| **1857** | Gregor Mendel starts experimenting with peas in his garden, leading to his laws of heredity |
| **1869** | Johann Friedrich Miescher discovers a biochemical in cells that he calls nuclein; today we know it as DNA |
| **1882** | Walther Flemming publishes a book that illustrates and describes cell division |
| **1890** | August Weismann discovers the importance of meiosis for reproduction and inheritance |
| **1903** | Walter Sutton determines that chromosomes may be the carriers of inherited characteristics; develops the chromosome theory of inheritance |

| | |
|---|---|
| **1921** | Thomas Hunt Morgan develops the idea that chromosomes carry genes, forming the basis of the modern science of genetics |
| **1947** | Gerty and Carl Cori receive the Nobel Prize for their discovery of anaerobic respiration (the Cori cycle) |
| **1951** | Rosalind Franklin begins using X-rays to study the structure of DNA |
| **1953** | Hans Adolf Krebs receives the Nobel Prize for his discovery of aerobic respiration (the Krebs cycle) |
| **1957** | Joan Wright Goodman begins her pioneering stem cell research |
| **1983** | Barbara McClintock wins the Nobel Prize in medicine for her work in genetics |
| **1986** | Rita Levi-Montalcini and Stanley Cohen share the Nobel Prize in medicine for identifying the nerve growth factor (NGF); Ernst Ruska wins the Nobel Prize for his invention of the electron microscope |
| **1995** | Christiane Nüsslein-Volhard receives the Nobel Prize for her research on genes that cause birth defects |
| **2003** | The Human Genome Project is completed; 99% of DNA is sequenced |
| **2006** | Elaine Fuchs publishes her research findings on stem cells in mice |
| **2008** | Researchers at Penn State University create an artificial cell in order to study the functions of the cell membrane and cytoplasm |

# Additional Resources

Camp, Carole Ann. *American Women of Science.* Berkeley Heights, N.J.: Enslow Publishers, 2001.

DuPrau, Jeanne. *Cells.* San Diego: Kidhaven Press, 2002.

Nardo, Don. *Cure Quest: The Science of Stem Cell Research.* Minneapolis: Compass Point Books, 2009.

Snedden, Robert. *Animals: Multicelled Life.* Oxford: Heinemann Library, 2002.

Stille, Darlene R. *Animal Cells: The Smallest Units of Life.* Minneapolis: Compass Point Books, 2006.

Stille, Darlene R. *Plant Cells: The Building Blocks of Plants.* Minneapolis: Compass Point Books, 2006.

## On the Web

For more information on this topic, use FactHound.

1. Go to *www.facthound.com*

2. Type in this book ID: 0756539641

3. Click on the *Fetch It* button.

FactHound will find the best Web sites for you.

# Index

## Kimberly Fekany Lee

Kimberly Fekany Lee earned her B.S. in chemistry from the University of Florida. She then studied axis formation in zebrafish to earn her Ph.D. in molecular biology from Vanderbilt University. Lee worked as a high school science teacher in Fort Lauderdale, Florida, before moving to the Chicago area. She is currently a freelance science writer and editor, residing in La Grange, Illinois. She is married and enjoys sharing her love of science with her three children.

## Image Credits